Jayne's Life Sentence

Jayne's Life Sentence

— The Shackles of Sexual Abuse —

By Jayne

authorHOUSE®

AuthorHouse™
1663 Liberty Drive
Bloomington, IN 47403
www.authorhouse.com
Phone: 1-800-839-8640

First published by AuthorHouse   02/20/2012

ISBN: 978-1-4678-8911-7 (sc)
ISBN: 978-1-4678-8912-4 (ebk)

Printed in the United States of America

Dedication

To my three little monsters, whose innocent
happiness lightens my heart.

To my husband who saved my soul.

Together they give my life the purpose and
direction it craves.

Introduction

THIS IS NOT MY ATTEMPT at a best seller or even a seller! It is simply a way in which I can put my life into some logical order.

By putting my thoughts and experiences down on paper it helps to clear the mind and know that my memories are not erased but filed away in a place where I can visit when I need to.

This may appear very strange. Surely if I could erase my memories then I would have cured myself. However if I deleted my true memories then my past would be a blank because to me a happy childhood and pleasant memories are a fantasy that I can't begin to accept as a possibility for me. I am too damaged.

I feel like a pack mule travelling along a narrow winding road. This is road I don't want to travel along, but ahead I see happiness and relaxation at the next bend. Therefore I forge ahead and do whatever is necessary to reach the bend and end this awful journey. However each time I near the bend my chance of happiness and relaxation dashes along the road ahead to the next turn. I am constantly travelling along life's path but at each twist in the road I have new challenges and direction to achieve peace. I have never yet been successful. This book is simply another stretch along my journey through life and recovery.

As a child my only wish was to escape my situation, then when I had escaped and was relatively safe from new onslaughts of abuse I wanted my abuser to be stopped as he had gathered new victims. I was almost on a crusade with the firm belief that by getting justice I could move on. And boy was I wrong about that.

Sure, I still feel going to court was right but it was not the end, merely the next stage. In truth the case almost brought on a nervous breakdown. I really thought this is it, I cannot cope anymore. I did not feel stronger or empowered. I felt weak and vulnerable.

After the court case, came my wonderful children. Three healthy and beautiful children. Sadly one little girl was destined for the arms of the angels. On the other side of the coin came post natal depression and a surge in my well established eating disorder.

Now I am at a place where I have learned to survive depression and taken pro active steps to tackle my weight issues.

It has also dawned on me that although I am getting to a better place in my life I am still running on the wheel and learning to accept that I may never step off.

I published this book to give others an insight into the mind of an abused child, so that they can help a child in their life. Unfortunately we probably all know someone who can be termed as abused or damaged. I also hope that other abused children who are now adults can relate to my experiences and realise that they are not alone.

They can see that abuse is real, it is serious, it is sadly very common and it is a life sentence with no chance of parole.

Before innocence was lost

I REMEMBER MY INNOCENCE AND open naivety as clearly as though it were yesterday. It is in such stark contrast to the rest of my life.

The images and memories I have are of a large and extended family that all laughed and fought in a safe environment.

I am the eldest in a family of four and had a score of cousins. I had two younger sisters, a baby brother, and my parents, close family ties with my maternal relations and a less gregarious relationship with my paternal family. Even at such a young age of six I knew there was a difference in my relations, i.e. their differing religions.

My mother who was a lapsed Catholic had herself quite a devout mother. My maternal grandmother whom I loved was always referred to as Mammy. I really loved Mammy. I felt sympathy for her as I sensed a lot of heartache and hurt. To me she was fantastic. She took me everywhere, sneaked me treats when I wasn't allowed, told me stories and protected me from my mother when I had misbehaved. She was my main source of safety and happiness. She made me feel good about myself. She made me feel special just because I was me. Something no one else has ever been able to do.

My highly intuitive senses were already at play by the age of six. Although they made me aware of impending trouble and anxiety they did not grace me with the knowledge of how to avoid such upsetting events.

I spent a lot of weekends and holidays with my maternal family. I enjoyed the change of running wild in a small town. I was free to be a child. Even misbehaving was ok here. It was expected and accepted as part of childhood. I was an exceptionally good child who had a *goody two shoes* personality.

I slept beside Mammy, I went to Chapel daily with her and I said my prayers at night with her. She instantly made me happy and Mammy was the personification of all that was right and good in the world. I'm sure as a person she was not perfect but to me her special granddaughter she was fantastic. I was deeply upset when she passed away when I was eleven. I found it difficult to accept that she was no longer around. I did not get *closure* as I was not allowed to see her on her death bed. From then on I replaced Mammy with her daughter, my aunt Peggy.

I was under no illusions as to Peggy's imperfections. She was an unmarried single mother of three, who ran quite a tight ship, but to me she was soft and gentle and again I had an unspoken knowledge that her failings in life were not a measure of her as a person but rather the product of a difficult and confusing adolescence. Peggy was like my unofficial mother. Someone I liked to please, hated to disappoint and someone who I admired for her inner strength, her tenacity and fight.

I am glad that before her very premature passing I had the opportunity to talk openly and honestly to her. I revealed my deepest darkest secret and she believed me instantly without a flicker of doubt. For that I loved her more than ever.

I still miss her daily and still pick up the telephone to call her. I take comfort in the knowledge that her spirit still is with me walking beside me through life. I see a lot of Peggy in my daughter, which I really enjoy. I feel that I am not alone in life. I am responsible for my children, my husband and my family circle. It is good to feel that some people like Mammy and Peggy are still looking out for me.

My relationship with my paternal grandmother was limited. I saw her regularly and she was never anything but decent toward me, however there was a distance that age and time simply could not bridge. We did not *click* at all. There was simply a superficial relationship that lacked any layer of emotion. I could quite easily have just been the next door neighbour's child. Again this I felt was because my father a good loyal Protestant had *lowered* himself to marry a Catholic Papist who had bred nothing but Catholic off spring.

I never questioned this attitude as there was no point and who really cared. I had Mammy and Peggy and they were all I needed. I didn't have the respect and admiration for my parents that a six year old should have. It was simple to me. They didn't deserve it.

My mother had been let down in life by her father. He abandoned her at the age of five. He had been a good loving father who had an alcohol problem. He made poor choices and his wife and children bore the brunt of it, in terms of shame and humiliation. I think the fact that there had been a mutual loving relationship made the separation very bittersweet. Mum was a selfish, immature woman who always had to be the centre of attention in relation to men. This stemmed from her deep seated insecurities and paranoid fear of abandonment. My father on the other hand had swathes of confidence, attitude and arrogance. Together they made a very volatile pairing.

Mum flirted, dad was jealous. Mum drank and became paranoid, dad drank and became violent. Mum was loose of the tongue and dad wandering with his eye and hands. Clearly, not a good combination.

Through the week mum and dad worked, we went to school and the normal home life ensued. Then came the dreaded weekend, I could never fathom why two people who were painfully aware that intoxication was the basis of their violent and hurtful relationship felt the overwhelming need to consume copious amounts of the stuff week after week.

Friday night began with my parents laughing and getting ready to go out. I was left to babysit. Finally, I would have a few hours of peace. I never felt lonely or scared watching my siblings, even though I was well below ten years old.

Every weekend I fooled myself into thinking that I had two happy parents who went out laughing and would come home in a similar fashion. The truth was that I was awoken about 3am by my mother screaming and shouting. Then there were the consistent warnings from my father, of which my mother took no heed. When he had listened to enough then her screams turned to pleas before he smashed her body once more. This was terrifying because my father was a strong well built man of 6ft 2in and my mother a small slight woman of 5ft 2in. Oddly, I was not concerned that my mother would be hurt but that my father would kill her and go to prison. Then what would become of me and my brother and sisters? I rather preferred the adage *better the devil you know*.

The next day was as always a *let's pretend day*. We children pretended not to see the bruises or smell the alcohol or even wonder why dad was in bed all day. Mum pretended we had been misbehaving so that she could dole out her residual anger and hurt from the night before. This would take the form of a good beating bestowed upon one or more of her chosen off spring. And so life in our household continued. Roll on Monday.

This may explain why I enjoyed school so much. I was clever and sailed through school work. The escapism was vital. The social side was not as easy. I was shy, secretive and feared making friends in case they could see my home life by looking in my eyes. If I did make friends would they want to come and stay? That was a risk I couldn't take.

I knew my home life wasn't great but I had school, Mammy, Peggy and my best friend Diana. Diana was my sister with only two years separating us. She accepted me and I admired her. We always were and still are two very different personalities, however we blend perfectly. Without Diana in my life I would be without my anchor. She has shared almost all of my life and is the one person who truly knows how I think and why I am the way I am. I don't have to explain to her she just gets it.

All in all my life had its problems but nothing that was insurmountable.

Little did I know then, but things were really going to get bad. I was to lose all hope and innocence forever.

My apocalypse

THE WORD *APOCALYPSE* MEANS LIFTING the veil of a misconception or simply a revelation. However I think that the word apocalypse strikes fear into people. There is an understanding that whatever the revelation is, it is going to be serious, negative and unnerving.

Most people view the end of the world and the revelation of God's divine plan as our apocalypse. Indeed for me as a six year old my apocalypse lived up to its' revered reputation.

Until now my life was relatively happy and I was an average child. Shy and socially inept but nevertheless optimistic, hopeful and forward thinking. Like any child I was self absorbed and bounced along through life from one event to another. I did not know the meaning of depressed, suicidal, guilty or ashamed. These were all emotions that would cascade over my whole being one summer evening. Emotions, still bathe my soul every day.

Until I was six years old I enjoyed a bedroom all to myself. Being the eldest child I felt that it was right I had my own space. I loved having a place for me and my things. Then my youngest sibling was born. It was a boy and as much as I loved him I had not made the connection, i.e. a boy would need his own room and I would have to share with my two younger sisters.

Saddened as I was I accepted the situation and took pleasure in the new bed my aunt had given me for my new room. My sisters both slept together in a double bed and I slept in my new single bed. I was happy because at least I still had my own bed if not my own room.

At this time in my life I enjoyed my father's company more than that of my mother's. Mum was cross, dictating and physically abusive towards us. Dad was calm, organised and never would hit us, (even though he hit my mother regularly). Dad would talk to us and more importantly listen to us. To mum we were simply the resented residue of a teenage pregnancy which thwarted her enjoyment of life.

It was a summer evening, still clear outside. My mother was not at home. Where she was I don't know. I don't even remember where my brother was but he was an infant. My room had a double bed for my sisters and a single for me, which was at the opposite end of the room. Dad was putting us to bed. This in itself was strange as usually we simply were told to go to bed. Bedtime routine, getting washed and having a night time story were an alien concept in our home. This was some fantasy that kids on television enjoy.

I had gotten into bed and turned to face the wall. I was settling into a sleep and the house was quiet, when my father whispered something inaudible in my ear and then crept into my bed. At that moment I felt a deep sense of insecurity and helplessness. Although I was unaware of why he was there or what his intentions were, I knew I was trapped that I had no escape. My body froze like ice and barely dared to breathe. He lay behind me with his arm around me. Then he slipped his hand down to my pants and reached inside. Inside I was screaming but not a peep did I make. It was over in a minute or two before he kissed my head goodnight then he simply left the room.

My mind was in a whirlwind. I was feeling physically sick yet it also seemed unreal. Whether I was in denial, in a blind panic or hoping it would never happen again I can honestly say that my life changed forever that summer evening. I was no longer a child; my father had in two minutes stolen my entire childhood and scarred the remainder of my life.

My soul is unwashed, dirty, damaged and flawed. Though I endlessly wash, live in denial, get angry, seek justice, be hypnotised, undergo cognitive behavioural therapy and meditate still my soul is deeply melancholy and daily, my anti depressants and I wander through my life as an onlooker. I am unable to truly feel emotion or bask in the happy home life I have created for my children. I am outside looking in and though I have tried every possible way in I am destined to remain a lonely outsider, a pretender in my own life. He has cheated me out of happiness, fun, a restful mind, self confidence and at times the will to live.

My new existence

AT FIRST I ACTUALLY BELIEVED that my father would realise that his actions were so wrong that they could never be repeated. I floated along on the dream for a few days until the inevitable happened again.

He must have realised my room was too crowded to take the risk, so instead he made it his business to get me on his own. As a mechanic who worked from home he had ample opportunity out in his garage store room. I had always been tinkering about in the garage so to refuse to go there would have been like holding up a red flag. Instead I continued my activities and put myself in the firing line.

For this I felt juxtaposed. On one hand here I was making myself available to be abused whilst simultaneously hoping that someone would save me. The mixture of fear and guilt can really fuck with your mind. Add in the fact I was barely seven and the damage is permanent and catastrophic.

The physical assault started with him touching me and sickeningly kissing me on the lips. I think this was the most awful part as I had to see his face up close and smell his rancid tobacco breath.

Then he escalated as is always the case. He made me touch him. He wanted me to masturbate him but obviously I didn't know how and my body froze each time he came near me. Then to repulse me even more he held my hand on his penis and went through the motions telling me to pay attention so that I would know for the next time. He talked to me like his peer, like an adult. Almost like, I was his new, inexperienced girlfriend. Whether he was living a fantasy or really believed his sick words I will never know.

When he had repeatedly warned me not to tell my mother because she would leave us, he started also came to me bed regularly at night. He had gained control of me and guaranteed my silence.

I would be asleep and then the nightmare would play out once again. I always pretended I was asleep so as to evade the bile provoking kiss. Imagine being awoken by your father's hands moving impatiently under the covers till he found your legs. Then he parted them and penetrated me with his fingers whilst masturbating at the side of the bed. It seems silly but I remember thinking of the mess he would leave on the carpet. When he was finished he casually got off the floor and mopped up his mess with some toilet roll. I actually felt quite triumphant when I pretended to sleep because I didn't have to place him in my mouth and taste him. The less active my role the more I could detach myself.

During my night visits I remember praying to God that my Mother would wake up to find him gone and go in search of her husband. It never happened.

Daytime opportunities were my father's speciality. My mother frequently ran errands and visited friends and family and my father was quick to volunteer my services with household chores and DIY. There were also the trips in the car with my father. These were very frightening because even if I had made a break for freedom or shouted for help no one would hear me. I was even more vulnerable. Daytime attacks were worse than nights as I was forced to carry out sexual acts and he would kiss me and ask me if I was enjoying it.

One Sunday morning my father was in bed well after lunch time. I was sent down with tea by my mother and told to waken him. Although I couldn't refuse I felt pretty safe because my mother was in the house and it was during the day. Yet again I was wrong. That day was one of the most physically painful days of the abuse. Amongst others my father had decided that it was time to rape his seven year old daughter in his marital bed whilst his wife and children were two rooms away. Perhaps the fear of being caught turned him on. I didn't feel trapped or scared that day because every part of my body was in agony as my father raped me. The pain was excruciating and I cried profusely. He never climaxed and told me not to feel bad that I couldn't satisfy him because although I was "too tight" it was growing and soon we could both enjoy it.

Take a moment to imagine a seven year old girl you know. Really picture her. Now think of her father, her protector raping her. Actually run through the process in your mind. If that makes you as an adult mentally disturbed and physically sick as it should, take a moment to walk in the child's footsteps. Once you complete this horror you may have an understanding as to why some people outright refuse to believe such testimony. It is so much easier to disregard the abuse of a child as exaggerated, made up or simply the evil imagination of a child, rather than accept the deeply disturbing truth. I feel it is the mind in self-preservation mode.

One time he told me he would make me enjoy it and would make me "cum". I was about 10 and hadn't a clue what the word meant. I was soon to find out. It was the first and last time he performed oral sex with his daughter. That day my body completely betrayed me. He had expected me to realise the joy of sex with your father and suddenly become a willing and eager participant.

At weekends my parents always left me alone to babysit whilst they went to local pubs and clubs, drank and fought. I really looked forward to my time alone. Some weekends when my parents had rowed before a night out, my mother would have left the house by the time my father arrived home. Being a jealous man it drove him crazy that mum was dressed and out on the tiles without him. When he was getting washed to go out, he would call me to get him the shampoo. Shampoo was another way of saying come to the bathroom, get naked, lie down on the bathroom floor and let me penetrate you with my fingers then masturbate and ejaculate over you. By this stage I had pretty much died inside and was numb.

I remember one rare occasion when my father came home before my mother after a night out. He ordered me into his room and quizzed me as to where my mother was. I explained I didn't know and that I had been asleep. This was 2 in the morning remember. He then began to violently shake me and talk to me as though I were my mother. He was completely irate and crazy. He slapped me hard across the face, one cheek at a time in such quick succession I almost passed out. I was crying hysterically. I couldn't even see straight. Then he told me he was sorry and that it was my mother's fault because she was out whoring. The beating was actually a good thing. It shocked me, woke me from my numbness and I could feel something again. Then just as quickly he plunged me into despair by touching me and making me give him oral sex whilst having to explain to him why I didn't want to. This episode was abruptly ended when a taxi arrived with my mother. Later that night I listened as my mother was beaten. Anger and resentment made me think that she deserved it because her actions that night had caused such horror for me.

I meander through the varying camps of thought. The first camp that my father wanted to increase the risk of being caught, second camp that he wanted to show off to me his complete control and power over me, or camp three that my mother knew off his activities and he wanted to rub my nose in it and show me that I had no escape. Whichever is true I will never know, but at night when he and my mother were going to bed he would call me into their bed and instruct me to lie in between them and have a talk about general things. No one was allowed under the covers just me. Whilst I lay there I was paralysed with fear. Fear of the abuse and fear that my mother would realise what was going on and blame me. During this time my father would fumble in my pants and penetrate me with his fingers and would make me masturbate him.

Money was tight in our home. Okay, there was always money for cigarettes and alcohol and new clothes for my mother, but as for regular food supply, clothing or activities for us children then no was always the answer. To palm me off my mother would tell me I would have to ask my father. Foolishly at the start I did. However when the reply that came back was that I had to do something for him first, I refused to blatantly prostitute myself and never asked again.

I still feel my stomach clench and a wave of shame when I think that my father simply instructed me on what he wanted and I did it. I had systematically gone through the process of avoiding him, pretending I was asleep, refusing and crying. All were futile. I quickly learnt to shut up, do as I was told and never refuse. Point blank refusal evoked immediate anger and outrage followed by physical abuse. Every avenue I tried was blocked. I wished at a very young age that I would go to sleep one night and never awaken. I am saddened to say that now happily married with three beautiful children, during dark times I still have that wish.

Daily survival and the loss of hope

FROM NOW ON I OPERATED purely in survival mode. Although at the time I didn't understand my behaviour, now I can clearly see a child focused on surviving a living nightmare.

Each day I stated with the futile hope that the sickening sexual incidents of the day before where somehow a blip or malfunction on my father's part. Today I would no longer be his prey but a normal child. By lunch this hope had swollen and just as it was about to come to fruition, my father's would crush any glimmer of hope or delusion that I had been holding onto.

Eventually I reconciled myself to the fact that hope was foolish and suffering was my lot in life. I accepted this and then sought out why I had been chosen for such pain. I was so engrossed in my attempts at avoiding my father coupled with trying to figure out why I was so bad, that I isolated myself.

At school I never made any attempt to make friends. I was a bad girl who deserved punishment. I had very few social skills and trusted no one. Children don't take kindly to the quite shy child. Instead they ignored me and later mentally bullied me. In a way my life at home was a sort of shield to their bullying, snipes and remarks because whatever they did to me it was nowhere near as cruel as my home life.

I threw myself into school work because it was logical and straightforward. If you work hard you stay out of trouble and do well. It is also a great mental escape.

If my odd behaviour and lack of a smile was noticed by other relations I never picked up on it. They all thought I was the perfect child. A quiet shy child, who worked hard at school, never answered back and carried out chores around the home. No one seemed to notice that this was abnormal for a child of my age.

I felt that if an adult looked at me right in the eye then they would see into my soul. I was undecided between them feeling pity for me and offering help or hating me for the evil child I really was. I don't know if I exhibited obvious signs of a poor home life or not, but if I did then no one intervened or asked if I was ok.

Even if they had asked I would only have been able to confirm or deny. I couldn't talk about the abuse because the words would have stuck min my throat and refused to have developed into meaningful sentences.

I wanted someone to see my suffering, ask no questions, immediately understand and take me somewhere safe. I wanted a miracle!

Onset of mental corruption and the eating disorder

MY ABUSE BEGAN WHEN I was seven. By the time I was eleven or twelve I was very depressed and withdrawn. I failed to find enjoyment in activities or events. I studied hard each day, carried out most household chores and then went to bed dreading my nightly caller. If the abuse took place during the day such as at weekends then I was actually relieved because I knew I could go to bed and sleep. Week nights were the worst. He had no opportunity to force himself upon me during the day and I went to bed almost paralysed with fear. I felt my breathing so loud and my heart race until my friend sleep came and took me briefly from the world. At this point I didn't care about myself at all. My past was gone, I felt I had no future and my only existence was daily torment. The stress I was under was like carrying around an actual weight. My body was weary physically and mentally.

We all find ways of coping. Up until this point I lived on a diet of self denial, flourishes of hope and a good salting of hard work. Around this time I discovered a new weapon for my armoury of self preservation. Eating!

Not normal eating but binging and eating in secret. There was a dual benefit from this behaviour. Firstly, whilst eating I was immediately transported to place where I hadn't visited in a long time, the land of relaxation. It felt so good. Secondly, as time went on I began to gain weight and was convinced that soon I would be so ugly and fat that my father would leave me alone. Instead, he bullied me and criticized me for being so greedy and fat. He hated me more and abused me more, almost like an extra punishment. That's when I realised that I needed to stop eating so much. Problem was that I couldn't. I had no other means of escape or relaxation and food hit the spot every time. I was so addicted that I even got up during the night to eat. I tried purging but I couldn't physically make myself sick.

I am now in my thirties and have never been able to resist the food addiction that I developed as a child. I tried every diet, hypnosis, exercise, starvation and fad diets. All failed. I realised that my eating was symptomatic of my mental state and that in order to resolve my eating addiction I needed to sort out my head. So then came counselling and cognitive behaviour therapy. These helped to a degree but not significantly.

The problem was that now I wasn't just fat, I was very unhealthy. At the age of 33yrs I pleaded with a bariatric surgeon for his help and he helped me. He advised me rationally on my options, the risks and benefits and the long term implications. I agreed to opt for bypass surgery. The best decision I ever made. I am no longer morbidly obese and I actually am healthy again. I still have all my demons, nightmares and mental scars, but now I simply can't eat my problems away, I have to deal with them, face them and work through them. I can only cope on a day to day basis, but that I can manage.

The child finally speaks

IT IS QUESTION I HAVE often heard—*why did he/she not tell someone?*

I am a little juxtaposed to that question. Indeed I can understand the question being asked, yet so angry at people's lack of understanding or empathy.

It is not their fault. These people are thinking logically and rationally, that is for a person who has never been abused in any manner. As victims of sexual abuse, domestic abuse or even substance abuse can attest the feeling of entrapment and shame is paralysing.

I felt that my father abused me not because he was a paedophile but that I had something wrong with me and this made him abuse me. In a way I obviously deserved to be abused. I had done something, said something or simply had something bad within me and my punishment was the sexual abuse.

When you feel you are to blame even in the slightest way, you want the problem to go away and never be exposed. Coping with the experience takes all your strength and you simply don't have anything left in order to deal with the fallout of your confession.

By the age of thirteen I was tired from avoiding my father, I had came to the conclusion that this was my life from here on in.

My will to live was slipping away and I was waiting and hoping for death. Death was more attractive than my life. I could be at peace with my granny and I would be able to rest.

My broken spirit meant that my cheery facade was flawed. I didn't carry it off as well. Through a few unusual answers and comments to my sister, I left it obvious what was happening. This may sound rare but my sister and I were very close and almost telepathic. We can finish each others' sentences and read so much from each others' tone.

Diana was the first soul my dirty secret became known to. Although she was two years younger she was brilliant. She never doubted me once. Her reaction was sympathy and empathy and that gave me such a sense of love and for a few moments I felt worthy to be alive.

I believe it was this experience that opened the floodgate. It gave me the confidence to dare to think that maybe others would also see the situation as unacceptable and somehow save me.

A few nights later at bedtime my mother told me to go and give my father a kiss goodnight. At this Diana and I exchanged glances and my mother immediately sensed something. However it is my strongly held belief that she picked up on the tension too quickly and worked out exactly what was going on with my father too easily, without me telling her. She asked all the questions and I simply responded yes or no. Right at that moment I felt completely crushed as I realised she knew, she knew all along, my mother knew her husband had been abusing her daughter and yet continued with her life.

I had some fairytale notion that when I finally gathered the courage to shatter our family's life by exposing my father, that my mother would be a mother and protect me. I would be safe.

The reality was so awful, so, so awful. My mother completely ignored me. She didn't ask questions or reassure me; in fact she never spoke to me for the rest of the night.

That was a long, tense night. My mother immediately went ballistic. She marched down to her bedroom where my father was in bed. She roared, shouted, cried etc. He in returned called me a liar and a whore. There were no words of regret or defence. What struck me sharply was that my mother was not distraught that her eldest child had been abused by her husband she was distraught because her husband had cheated on her. It was at this point I realised how far my mother fell short of my fairytale image of how my mother would save and protect me.

All night the rowing, shouting and banging continued. Eventually I fell asleep through nervous exhaustion. When I awoke the next morning my stomach was in knots and I felt like throwing up. I had been abused, and then I had asked for help, war had broken out and now I was going to have to expose myself to the strewn battlefield of emotions.

If I had anywhere to run I would have. I remember thinking about going to the local children's home as a means of escape but if I left who would protect my other sisters. If nothing else at least my suffering was keeping them safe. I couldn't simply abandon them.

I hesitantly went into the living room. My father was still in bed and my mother was cleaning out the fire. She looked up at me and her eyes were hard and defensive, there were no tears, no smiles no reassurances. I sat down and she began to talk. She proceeded to ask me if I wanted to go to the police. I said yes. She told me simply that that was not going to happen. She wasn't going to let *me* shame the family and destroy her reputation. She continued on to ask why had I let it happen, why didn't I stay out of his way and why did I lead him on. I remember feeling so dirty and ashamed. My mother told me it was my fault and I was going to ruin her life in the process. I was to keep quite. My father had told her that if it became public knowledge that he would kill himself by jumping over a steep hillside or cliff edge that was in the area where he worked at the time. My mother said that she wouldn't have this on her conscience. That was the end of discussion that day.

Life went on as usual between my mother and father and I was in a state of shock and abandonment. Around that time I was very sensitive to others commenting on what a nice family we all were and how we children were so lucky to have our parents because other kids had awful parents. I felt like I was actively participating in the facade by my silence. I wondered why the world couldn't see the real people I has for parents.

My mother was a selfish woman who abused alcohol, flirted outrageously, had affairs, physically abused her children, ignored her child being raped and had a vicious temper.

My father also abused alcohol, beat my mother regularly, raped me, had affairs and was a petty thief and bully.

Thirteen was the age when suicide became an option. Although baptised I was never take to Sunday services. Perhaps it was because of the Catholic/Protestant relationship my parents had or maybe as with other things, it would have been too much effort for my mother. Somehow though I believed there was a God and that if I committed suicide it would be a terrible sin and I would never go to heaven. That belief in God and the wrongness of suicide in God's eyes was a barrier for me. I wanted to escape my life so badly. It was school and home with a few hours work in a local shop. There were no youth clubs, visits to friends, afterschool clubs or activities. God forbid that we children might actually have had fun or enjoyment.

Going to work was an escape of sorts. Yes I was out of the house and meeting new people and escaping my suicidal thoughts. However I worked for £1/hour and this added up to

£11 per week. Out of that my mother took at least £5 for fuel and that caring father of mine would occasionally lift me from work and of course stop off en route home. Every day of work I feared in case he lifted me. I would walk over to the car with legs like lead, a pounding heart and bile rising.

Guilt, fear, shame and self loathing —the emotional residue of abuse

ABUSE CONJURES UP THE OBVIOUS: fear, pain, hurt, entrapment and survival. These feelings are readily apparent to any reasonable person when imagining themselves as a victim of abuse. I don't have any hang-ups about being labelled as a victim, because that is what I am. However being a victim should not and will not define me as a person. As well as being a victim of abuse, I am also a mother, a wife, daughter, a sister, an aunt, a friend, a colleague and a God fearing person. I cannot allow one awful aspect of my life ride rough shot over all the good and pollute any future I am to have. I owe it to myself to be the best that I can, if not for me then for the happiness and stability of my children, which mean more to me than anything. If I rear three happy, well adjusted children who can look in the mirror and feel content, then I will have achieved my greatest goal in life.

To be a good mother, wife and individual would be my highest accolade.

I have accepted that I will never be truly happy. Remove the bravado, the sarcasm and the willingness to help others and there will always be a deep and vast black hole at the centre of by being with a broken spirit overhanging.

Guilt:

I will always feel guilty for allowing my father to abuse me. This statement defies logic and reasoning as I was only a young, innocent and vulnerable child. I know this with my head but my heart and soul seek to punish and atone.

Fear:

I live in perpetual fear. Fear that once again someone or something will place me and my emotions in their hands and do with me what they wish. I am a self confessed control freak with a large helping of OCD. I do things my way when at all possible because this is how I keep safe. To onlookers I appear bossy and judgemental and a bit of a tyrant. If only they could feel my heart beating or hear the whoosh of blood in my ears whenever I feel that I am no longer in charge of a situation. To lose that control and structure is to be transported back to being a fragile child being raped by her father.

Over reacting?

Yes.

Any less real to me?

No.

Shame:

I have often seen on television and in life the child who denies they have been in the cookie jar yet brandishing a rather brown stained face. I am that child. I go through the motions of everyday life just as anyone does but I know they can see past my facade. Written all over my face is that I ruined my parents marriage, I made my father bad, I wasted police time, I am a nasty, lying little whore. They can see my blackened soul. I sometimes think that the abuse is my huge, angry inflamed port wine stain that the entire world can see no matter how much foundation I wear.

Self Loathing:

Ambivalence comes to mind at this point. On one hand I am a real plain Jane who makes no effort to look good. I overeat, I don't style my hair or apply make-up, my clothes would suit my granny and I feel depressed about my physical appearance. On the other hand when I make an effort with my hair and clothes or apply some make-up then I feel that I am prostituting myself to the world.

I sit at a function and feel so uncomfortable in my own skin that I wish I could run away. I want to be carefree and have a drink and a dance but my body won't allow it. It will not take any risk whatsoever of being noticed and violated again. I have over time tried to be more social and I come away feeling like a fool. Every laugh I hear is at my expense. Every cross word aimed at my actions. Life is so stressful that I want to retreat into my shell and be left in solitary confinement. Yet once there I can't bear to be alone with my memories and constant thinking and questioning. To use one of my husband's phrases, I am like a dog chasing its tail.

Anyone, whom knows an individual that is or has been a victim of abuse, never be fooled. Look beyond the awkward smile, look at the eyes and please don't be judgemental or off hand. I have noticed that once people learn of your abuse, they either disbelieve you and run a mile or move closer and try with the greatest of intentions to 'help' you. They want to fix you. There is no fixing an adult who was a sexually abused child. The damage is irreparable. I think this is the hardest thing for my husband to accept.

My personality, my confidence and my quality of life was altered beyond recognition at the age of seven when my father crept into my bed.

My first glimmer of light—Raymond

"A GOOD HEART THESE DAYS is hard to find". These words from a song are very true. I was lost in a dark deep place and no one was able to reach me. I had all but given up hope of surviving when along came my lifeline. Lifeline is an understatement. I remember Raymond, immediately made me feel good inside. I hadn't felt that in years. I was slowly slipping away when this strong, gentle soul decided to notice me and my suffering.

Raymond was so easy going. He was funny and happy and innocent. I can honestly say that after 15yrs I haven't detected a bad fibre within his being. Sure he drives me nuts at times with his messiness but if that is all I have to complain about I am a very lucky girl.

Raymond saw me for me and liked what he saw. It took me a long time to accept that. Raymond was an extreme contrast to my father—in looks, personality, intelligence, work ethic and morals.

Most of all Raymond's gentleness made me feel safe. That was a feeling that I craved and clung to. To feel safe meant that I could relax and unclench my whole body.

After a few months I realised that I could actually survive my home life, I could have a life of my own and attain some level of normality and perhaps even eventually be happy!

I have always been a very truthful person. Lies made me feel uneasy and stressed. Playing mind games was my parent's speciality and I was not a fan. Bearing this in mind I decided that after four months with Raymond he deserved to know the real me, warts and all. I knew that any revelations I made could threaten or end the relationship but I needed Raymond to beware of the situation. If we were to have a future it needed to be built on honesty and trust.

My worst fear was that Raymond somewhere in the recesses of his mind would wonder how I had let it happen or was dramatising the situation. Thankfully my fears were unfounded.

Raymond was so shocked that a father could commit such atrocities with his own child. He admitted that he felt an anger and sadness that was unknown to him. He was also very concerned about my immediate safety. His love for me never flickered and he believed, understood and accepted me. It was at this point I knew that I truly loved and respected him and a deeper bond was forged.

From that point onwards our relationship was more focused on a long term relationship hopefully resulting in marriage. We both agreed to wait till university was over and I had a job before moving in together.

Our plans came to fruition and we moved in, got married and had three beautiful children. I feel blessed.

Life is good, now let's destroy it

SO LET'S SEE WHERE I am at now. Childhood was good, childhood destroyed, abandoned by my mother emotionally, mental issues and feelings of despair, then hope and safety with Raymond. A bit of a mixed bag really. One would be forgiven for thinking hooray! Life's hurdles have been overcome and life is happy ever after. Well one would be wrong.

I had left university and was working so Raymond and I decided to set up home. Neither of us had money but a loan and a lot of DIY meant we lived meagrely but happily. All I can remember is that my life was on the up; I had escaped from home and was building a life with a wonderful person. This was all I could ever have hoped for. Then as I begin to relax and uncoil from years of fear and pain the floodgates open. My mind and body is safe and suddenly all my past experiences, hurt, terror and fear come cascading into my lovely safe relationship. I was completely powerless to stop it. The adrenalin flow had dried up and I was going to have to face my past whether I wanted to or not.

My emotions were a rollercoaster that I was unable to halt or slow. In my mind I knew I was irrational, teary, cross, depressed and completely unreasonable but I couldn't lift my finder of the self destruct button. I knew I could only keep the

Genie in the bottle for so long but never intended Raymond to be caught in the cross fire.

I still knew I loved him and hoped he loved me but beyond that I had lost control. I wasn't cross I was irate and felt that I was going insane.

Raymond thought it was living together but I knew otherwise. I realised that if I didn't get some help then I would lose Raymond.

First I explained the situation to Raymond. He listened and understood but was unsure if I could work through my issues. He was there for me but only if I sought some help.

I hated my job and set about changing that. I signed up for counselling, got self help books and eventually went to the doctor for something to level out the emotional roller coaster I was on. I also went to court to prosecute my father for raping and abusing me.

Raymond knew I was determined to get better but didn't know if I could conquer the demons within. Thankfully he stood by me till I crawled out the other end.

Looking back it all makes sense really. I couldn't deal with my situation whilst at home because I was in survival mode, then when I could put distance between me and the past and feel safe having left survival mode I went into reaction mode, then recovery.

It was a process that was inevitable I am sorry Raymond had to be caught up in it all and glad that he was strong enough for the both of us.

The court case

I HAD STARTED TRAINING FOR my new career which was very intensive and away from home with Raymond. Stress levels were high. I had worked hard to gain my place on the training course for the job of my dreams. I had the partner and the home now came the job. It was a bit of a double edged sword though. The more I achieved and progressed throughout my life the more I could lose and the further I could fall.

Since my mother's abandonment of me emotionally at 13yrs old we had a very strained relationship. My mother begrudgingly played nice and I reluctantly allowed her to. The relationship was strained at best and a complete sham at worst. She hated the fact that I held her accountable and I hated the fact that she blamed me. So we danced around each other at family occasions and celebrations and kept a respectable level of communication.

At this stage I am progressing and making headway. Then my mother in her usual selfless and caring way (not), informs me that she has informed the local police of my father's abuse towards me. She quickly adds that I have to go and make a statement that night. Again I have been sent into a whirlwind of thoughts, emotions and fears.

On one hand I strongly believe that my father should pay for his crimes and that I should have an integral part to play. On the other hand I know that I am being manipulated and bullied. My mother is using me as her trump card against my father's from whom she is now separated. I knew not to expect any support or care throughout. When I was 13yrs old and needed her to go to the police to help me, she blamed me and ignored my call for help. Yet now when she wants to annihilate her ex husband I can then be useful.

Somehow from somewhere I got the strength to go to the police station with my mother who acting the part of distraught mother so well. Making the statement was actually easier than I thought. I simply pretended to be telling someone else's story. I completely detached myself. I pushed the whole thing to the back of my mind until the day of the court case arrived.

I couldn't hide any longer.

My mother

MY MOTHER IS A VERY vague title. I want to discuss my mother and how her personality was shaped as a child and adult. I am not trying to assassinate her character but explore the person she was and how those traits influenced her mothering ability.

My mother was born into a happy family. She was the youngest of three girls and suitably spoiled. Both parents had an active role in the girl's lives and they mulled along nicely. My granny had some tragedy with children. Her second pregnancy was twins who were born prematurely and died hours after being born. When my mother was three she contracted meningitis and was very ill indeed. Luckily she pulled through fine. My mother blames her temper and anger on the meningitis, I beg to differ.

When my mother was about six or seven her father abandoned her family and ran away to Scotland with another woman. My mother's father was an alcoholic. Yes he went to work each day but was in the pub at other times. What was so awful for my mother was that she had been enjoying a happy childhood. She had parents who never fought, enough clothes and food, an extended family network and parents who loved her. Suddenly she was plunged into an entirely different existence. Her family barely had enough to eat, relied on handouts to

survive and witnessed their happy mother crying night after
night. The shame at that time in the 1960s was immense. I don't
think my mother ever got over being abandoned by her father.
She was a happy loved girl without a care in the world and then
she became the town news, a shamed embarrassed and hurt
child.

At that time I believe my mother decided to look out for
herself. She had to be tough to survive. Throughout her teenage
years she had a number of boyfriends whom treated her very
well. Then in about 1974 she had the unfortunate meeting with
my father. I don't know what the attraction to him was. He
wasn't a looker, money was tight, he was the wrong religion
and early into the relationship he started to be very jealous.

This relationship progressed into an abusive one. Both my
mother and father were jealous and flirtatious with a fondness for
alcohol. Never a good cocktail. My father's jealousy developed
into physical abuse and both he and my mother had affairs.
Somewhere around the two year mark of the relationship and
I was conceived. Their relationship was so bad that my father
asked her if the child was his.

My granny and aunt begged my mother not to marry such
a brut. Stubborn as ever my mother married my father moved
in together and had three more children. My mother was not by
any means a shrinking violet. She had spirit, friends, family and
a wide social network and work contacts. Why she thought an
adulterous wife beater was good enough for her I think stems
from her deep rooted insecurities and feelings of unworthiness
when her father left her.

I believe if my mother had married a civil decent man then
she could have worked through her problems and felt good
enough to love herself and her children. She was a victim of
circumstance and poor decision making. My grandfather may
have abandoned my mother but she also abandoned me. I just

hope that I have put a break in the cycle and do not damage my children.

From a very young age 2-3yrs I can remember the arguments and later the physical beatings weren't hidden. As a child I can remember that nearly every Friday night my parents went out socialising. Alcohol, cigarettes, mother's new fashions, tans and socialising were always on the agenda. I remember thinking that I needed new shoes or clothes or a decent school bag yet there never was any money. At times the cupboards were bare and school trips or extra were a no-no. I could never understand why there was no money for us children but abundance for the adults. Even at that stage in life I knew my mother was selfish. I can't say the same about my father as he did regularly give her money. Money was my mother's god.

From my knowledge my mother was never beaten as a child by either parent yet she beat us quite badly. My mother did not dole out a punishment for a wrong-doing; she gave beatings when she was stressed and angry. I have always believed my mother resented having children and beat us as punishment for existing. By a beating I mean she would slap our faces, pull our hair and ears, nip us, even bite us occasionally, slap and punch our bodies, kick us and degrade us by telling us we were stupid, fat or ugly. I don't think she could cope with her situation but wouldn't ask for help. To the outside world my mother had a clean, modern house with four well mannered children and a smile for all. School and staying with my granny were my escapes as a child.

My mother's life was more important than ours. We did occasionally have a babysitter. I don't remember when that stopped, but I do know that from seven onwards I was the main babysitter. I remember my brother was just a baby when I was seven and I changed his nappies and gave him midnight feeds. By the way the nappies then weren't disposable!

Our parents would go out for the night and leave four children home alone with a strict warning not to leave the house because the neighbours will get us taken away. They usually came home about two or three in the morning for a fight. IF I intervened I got hit as well and from I was 13yrs old my mother would always bring up the abuse to me when drunk to tell me it was my fault and attack me verbally. Sometimes when morning came they were still not home. My parents also left us alone for full days. We were left at home, not allowed out and a lot of the times with no meals. I use to make jelly simply because it was all I could find.

I remember Fridays being pay day for my father. When we lifted him from work we would go to the chip shop. My parents got whatever they wanted and we four growing children had to share one bag of chips. If we asked for anything else we were told how ungrateful we were and that when we had our own money then we could buy what we wanted.

As a child I knew my parents were poor at the job. I did all the housework until the age of 13yrs when I toned it down. From then I really hated my mother for abandoning me. If I could avoid being nice to her then I would. Birthday cards were always basic. The thought of sending a card to my mother saying how great she was simply sickened me.

I remember around the age of 15 or 16 I told my mother that I hated her and why. She was shocked and cried a lot. She was actually really hurt but never made any attempt to improve the relationship. I no longer appreciated anything she done for me; instead I tried to get as much from her as possible in terms of money etc.

It wasn't until my father left my mother for another woman when I was around 20yrs old that my mother began to see her children as a comfort rather than a pest. At this time my mother really did try to get closer with me, but by know I couldn't stand being in her presence. It wouldn't have mattered at that stage if she had given me the world, it still wouldn't have been enough. I wanted her to acknowledge what she had done and how she had treated me. I wanted an apology, a heartfelt apology. It didn't present itself.

Rachael

I FIND MYSELF IN AN awkward position each time a stranger or new acquaintance enquires if I have any children. If I say I have three, then I feel that I am ignoring Rachael or somehow ashamed of her. If I were to say four and explain that one has passed away before birth the conversation would quickly come to a close and that person would avoid the emotional neurotic woman at all costs.

Rachael was my second child, a very wanted and planned child as were all my little monsters. However right from the time I discovered I had conceived I knew in my heart the pregnancy would never come to fruition. I have always had a sense for impending events or tragedies. I knew instinctively with each pregnancy the sex of the life I was carrying and could see their little face at birth. With Rachael I simply couldn't look forward to her birth, I knew I would never cradle my daughter. I employed logic and rationale to calm my emotions and ignore my gut instincts. This worked well until at 6weeks I went to the toilet and discovered I had passed blood. I knew then that Rachael would never meet me in this world. I completely freaked out. I cradled my son and went into a strange rocking motion. I called Raymond who thought I was overreacting and there was probably a reasonable reason. His advice was to get a professional opinion. I contacted the midwife and explained the situation. I had a scan booked and was told to come ahead to the midwife and get all my bloods etc done. I knew I was wasting my time going through the motions with the midwife. The scan date came and I was terrified. I went on my own as it was the only way I could hold it together. I had prepared myself for the news that I had indeed suffered a miscarriage. To my amazement and confusion I was shown the screen with my baby's little sac and the pregnancy was still in progress. Although happy with the news I knew deep down that all was not well. I was in mourning for the loss off my child, but Raymond, the midwife, doctors and family were all reassured by the scan. I was so confused I felt I was going mad. All my instincts screamed that by little girl was leaving me whilst all the scans and tests told me otherwise. I got a scan every fortnight for the next six weeks and even saw the baby's heartbeat but the little sac was not getting any better. I trudged on through until my twelve week hospital scan. I had actually begun to relax a little once I saw the heartbeat flutter like a butterfly.

Again I went to the scan alone and was seen by an older doctor whom I hadn't met throughout my last pregnancy. When he performed the can he coldly and unemotionally told me that there was no baby. No softening of his voice or breaking the news gently or even offering any words of sympathy. The manner in which I was told was as hurtful as the information itself. I believed the doctor as he had confirmed my gut instincts, but he was dismissing me as a silly woman who thought she was pregnant. I explained that only two weeks ago the scan showed the heartbeat. He told me definitely not and walked away from me. Not only had I lost my child but her existence was being denied. I found that so very hurtful. By baby had a soul and was not a figment of my imagination. I cried uncontrollably the whole way home and couldn't seem to stop. Seeing wee Mark when I got home made me kick into mothering mode when his needs came before mine. Although Mark was so unaware his presence helped so much.

I was informed that I would need and operation to remove the remaining foetal tissue from my womb. The thought of scraping my child's remains from my body was too much to take in. I couldn't comprehend losing all traces of Rachael so swiftly. The operation was necessary to avoid infection and to help with future healthy pregnancies. I opted for a date two weeks away. In that time Raymond and I took a few days away to be on our own. I needed that time to untangle my emotions and say goodbye to Rachael.

I am happy to say that the hospital staff couldn't have been nicer and more sympathetic to my situation. I really felt looked after. It was heart warming when I learned that my baby's little body would not be incinerated but instead kept, looked after, placed in a little white box and buried with a dignified service at the graveyard.

The funeral was such a comfort. Raymond and Mark accompanied me. Mark was only a baby himself but I felt it important that we attend Rachael's funeral together as a family to say goodbye. Although the miscarriage was a huge loss for me I accepted that for Raymond a child is never real until the birth. He couldn't feel the morning sickness of bond with a little life that was not growing inside him. Raymond knew that I was terribly upset and understood that the loss was very different for me. He may not have felt what I did but he cared for me and gave me the love and support to carry me through.

I named her Rachael instinctively. She just felt like a Rachael. I have always been a fan of fortune tellers and after Rachael passed I also went down the road of clairvoyants. I know many people are of the belief that such abilities don't exist but I am a believer and have experienced psychic episodes myself. The clairvoyant conveyed to me that children who pass away grow up in heaven. My little Rachael was a little girl with an infectious laugh and was being looked after by my granny. That gave me a really warm feeling because if I were to choose anyone to love and care for a child it would be my granny.

I have told my children about their sister and I take comfort from not hiding her away like an unwanted memory.

I was shocked by how much Rachael's loss affected me. I can say with certainty that until you experience a miscarriage you won't fully appreciate the depth of feeling you experience for an embryo that has only been with you for a few weeks.

If you know someone who has had a miscarriage be sure that their loss is real and the baby they have lost is a person with a name and maybe even a little personality.

Me, depression and food

THROUGHOUT MY CHILDHOOD I WAS a survivor a fighter and I battled on. It was a continual cycle of adrenalin and fear fuelled emotional stress. I was embroiled in an ongoing traumatic situation. Each day was another battle or struggle; there was no time to reflect on the situation. When each day is different with no routine you never know where you are, where you are going or if you even want to survive it. There is never time to reflect because you are never in a safe and secure place to reencounter your memories and demons. I don't drink and have never taken drugs but boy do I understand why others do. If I have the opportunity or resources to partake then I would have to escape.

When a war is over, onlookers seem to think that's the job done, let's move on with life. Well sorry but that couldn't be further from the truth. It is only after a battle or war when you have limped or crawled to safety that you can assess the damage. When I escaped my home life, met my husband and battled a court case then I finally sat down breathed and surveyed the scars.

Let's just say it wasn't pretty. I hated myself. I was fat, ugly, and moronic and couldn't stand my own company. I felt ashamed to be a part of the world, but like all good pretenders I put on my public face, went to work and laughed at all the right times. I now realise that I wasn't hiding from others I was hiding from myself.

I never actually saw the depression coming. I believed that if I had survived until now in life without being depressed or mentally ill then nothing would tip me over. How wrong was I?

Depression was to be one of my closest friends. Each life experience was a small weight on my shoulders and over time they built and built until my shoulders collapsed and gave way. After losing Rachael I had no more fight in me. I just wanted to rot away in a corner. I went to the doctor and finally crumpled. I had to desist with the act and admit that I was depressed and in order to take care of my children I needed drugs. It was a last ditch attempt to cope. I had tried cognitive behavioural therapy, counselling, self help books and hypnotherapy. I didn't want to use medication because I wanted to prove that no matter what my father did to me, I was stronger, I was unbreakable. Now every morning when I reach for my happy pills it reminds me that my father has won and I have lost. That hurts.

I disgusted myself and then comfort ate. I wouldn't just comfort eat I would binge continuously but I never purged. I wasn't bulimic that was my mother's speciality; instead I was a big fat greedy binge eater.

I wasn't hungry in the slightest. In fact the food made me feel nauseous and bloated and tired. I ate to kill the pain and fill the aching gaping hole inside my soul. Binge eating was my own personal way to punish myself further.

I realised that like the depression I needed help with my eating disorder. Yet again daddy dear had left me with yet another reminder of his fathering ability or rather inability.

So after, dieting pills, every diet on the planet and more cognitive therapy and hypnosis I resigned myself to fact that I needed drastic help. I was now seriously overweight and starting to develop health problems.

I had a few pound saved and decided that a gastric band would be the way forward. It could be removed if necessary and wasn't as dangerous as a gastric bypass. So I was honest about my decision and my family who had witnessed my struggle with food gave me their full support. Raymond also gave his support because he realised I had a serious problem that was affecting my health and had tried everything I could think of. It was a great effort for me as I had to arrange childcare, fly to Birmingham and back on my own and then recover from the operation

Naively in keeping with the honesty theme I decided to let my in laws know my plans. Once again I had fooled myself into believing they were normal reasonable people, and since I was paying for the operation and arranging my own child care they couldn't possibly have a problem. Once again they rejected me out of hand as the crazy woman who is always causing a fuss. They were so forthcoming in saying "I told you so" when the gastric band failed horribly and to be removed.

My mother, take two

THROUGHOUT MY CHILDHOOD MY MOTHER has given me no indications that she loved me, none. Then her abandonment of me at the age of thirteen confirmed that she was a heartless selfish woman and I was no more than an inconvenience that she had been lumbered with.

However it was her frog marching me to the police to report my father's sexual abuse that drove the last nail into the coffin. She pushed me forward as a means to punish the man that left her. That wasn't revenge enough, she told anyone who would listen about the abuse and how badly *she* had been affected. At one point she tried to force me to go public with the abuse to tabloid papers. This would have served the dual purposes of public humiliation for my father and money and sympathy for her.

By now I was sickened by how nasty she was. It was when my Jenny was born in 2006 that I simply couldn't take anymore. The sheer sight of her made me angry. My mother was still making my life painful to experience.

I didn't want by anger and negative feelings to be expressed towards my children. She may have helped destroy my childhood but not that of my children. I couldn't protect myself but there was no way in hell she would ever harm by children. My mother had also become very dependent on alcohol. She and her toy boy partner were drinking most nights and it showed physically. Combine the alcohol, the chain smoking and the bulimia and you got a very ill looking woman with a stinking attitude. She had become an embarrassment and I needed her out of my life.

It was in autumn 2006 that I penned a letter to my mother and left it at her home. I made it clear that although I wished her health and happiness in life, I could no longer allow her to form part of my life. I explained the pain she caused, what I held her responsible for, her lack of remorse and not to make contact with me in any way shape or form. Thankfully she obliged and made no contact.

The relief and freedom I felt was immeasurable. I was free from my childhood constraints and could at last live my life instead of surviving it.

Without the irritation of my mother I began to deal with my past and to explore what I was feeling and why. I did a lot of soul searching, analysis and reflection. During that time I learnt to forgive. I have no control over my memories and don't feel that I will ever forget my childhood but I have been grated the gift of forgiveness. I want to be clear, I have not given anyone the gift of forgiveness to free them from guilt, but I have been given the ability to forgive from God and that has set me free.

As I began to unravel my emotions and deal with my issues, (of which there are many!), I also began to forgive my mother and more than that I began to miss having a mother. Although I didn't want my old mother back, after two years I did want a mother. My granny and my aunt who were both mother figures had died and I needed a mother. Nature seemed to kick in and I actually longed for a mother. Rational thought brought me to investigate through family what type of person my mother was now. I learned that she had given up drinking and was still with the same partner. Her life seemed stable. I began to toy with the notion that perhaps mum and I could have a relationship. I was very apprehensive. I didn't want to yoyo back and forward, speaking then not speaking etc. I had my own emotion and those of my three young children to consider. I discussed the issue with my husband, my sisters and brother. It was during a telephone conversation with my brother that I heard my mother talking in the background. It was at that moment the brain was taken over by the heart and the thought *I want my mummy* resonated. My mind had been made up; I would try to communicate with my mother.

I organised a meeting through family and my mother and I both cried. I explained why I needed the separation and why I wanted her back in my life. Mum expressed her regret of past decisions and made a genuine and sincere apology for discarding me all those years ago. We agreed on a fresh start, leaving the past behind and moving forward. I am pleased to say that I have never regretted either the decision to stop communications with mum, nor the resuming of lines of communication. I have a mother would doesn't drink, is interested in me and my family and most importantly a mother whom I fell loves me.

I don't want to ever meet my father again in this life or the next but I have forgiven him for what he has done to me and I have untied that burden and let it float away. I no longer hate him or wish him dead. Recently he had cancer and then a heart attack and I felt sorry for any person to be faced with such illnesses. I didn't for a moment take any delight in his suffering, and I'm glad about that.

Extended Family

What is the difference between in-laws and outlaws?
Outlaws are wanted!

I HOPE THAT SETS THE tone for the rest of the chapter. My parents were to put it nicely the ogres of my childhood, and extended or related family Peter and Winnie are the ogres of my adulthood.

In fact Raymond's parents Peter and Winnie, his sister Sharon and his brother Alan all need mental help. Boy do they have issues, all mixed together wide pride and snobbery. My husband was either adopted or extremely talented and deflected all the negative genes. Raymond is such a helpful, thoughtful and caring man. He is a gentle giant and they are well certifiable.

Where oh where will I begin. Let's go way, way back to the beginning and start with Sharon. I met Sharon at the local Grammar school. I knew from the outset that she was a strange entity. I found it difficult to figure her out or know what made her tick. I thought new school, new people, what the hell! It was during a night out with Sharon that I met Raymond. Instantly there was a spark and I was quite besotted. Becoming a friend of Sharon's had really paid off. As far as I can gather in Sharon's mind I was her friend and Raymond was her brother. We were support networks and relationships that Sharon had, however she was vehemently opposed to Raymond and I dating. The reaction was immediate. In her own way she explained that I had stolen her brother from her and Raymond had taken her friend from her. Sharon felt that we had somehow cheated on her and for that crime we would be made pay.

She had a divide and conquer strategy. As I am happily married to Raymond, Sharon's plan wasn't very effective. The plan was to reveal to me the *real* Raymond. The prostitute using, alcoholic, gambler who was the family's embarrassing yokel. Listening to this was all a little surreal. The Raymond I knew worked hard, had a few one night stands, went out with friends once a week and never gambled. Anyhow I decided to let her vent her frustrations and not wanting to rock the boat I simply nodded at all the right times and listened. Sharon was outraged and in disbelief when I informed her that I would judge Raymond as I found him and I was very happy with him.

Plan B was then put in motion. Sharon informed Raymond that I was a scummy, lower-class, IRA supporter who was only after his money.

Luckily for Raymond and me we talked, we communicated very well and there were never any secrets. Raymond was hurt by his sister as he thought they had a good relationship. In truth he couldn't quite believe her unfounded allegations. Surely it is wrong to be romantically jealous of your brother and friend dating.

Time rolled on and plan C came into play. Plan C was to turn the family against me with lies, insults and a series of public interrogations.

Obviously she couldn't cheat with Raymond so instead she tried to make me cheat on him. Her attempts at sabotage were all futile. She did however have her mother on side. Winnie didn't need to believe her daughter to be on her side, she is always on Sharon's side no matter how ludicrous the situation.

Sharon acted like Raymond's wife and treated me like the mistress. She huffed and threw tantrums when he took me out, went to graduations with me or even mentioned my name.

My name could no longer be mentioned in the household as it was offensive to Sharon. Instead of her mother telling her to wise up, she backed her to the hilt. My solution would have been to confront Sharon and Winnie, sort it out and move on. Raymond however would do anything he could to avoid an argument. I decided it was his family so we would handle it his way. His way was to allow himself and me to be their doormat. So many times I cried with hurt or frustration, bit my lip and at other times laughed at madness of the situation.

To top it all off Sharon still demanded that she and I go out together every Saturday night so that she could get a man.

The expression *fur coat and no knickers*, would describe Sharon very well. She was an educated, tall, blonde girl who ran about spending daddy's money and looking down upon the world beneath her, yet she would take strange men to daddy's jeep on a Saturday night, strip bullock naked and have her way with them. Meanwhile I was left alone at the bar asking myself how I had ended up here again.

Sharon was very strange in the choosing of a man. She was quite good looking and I'm sure would have had no trouble getting a date, however she actively targeted men that were in relationships already. Sharon wasn't interested in the man himself; instead she was determined to prove that the male in question wanted her more than his current partner. Therefore she was better than other women and foolishly believed she could have any man she wanted. She basically prostituted herself.

Eventually she met a very nice man McCay whom she described as old, boring and tight (with cash). Sharon said he would be a fill in or a man to do until she found someone her equal. She completed her teaching degree whilst having numerous emotional outbursts and paranoid thoughts. Her mother mollycoddled her through her degree.

All the time she dated McCay she two timed continuously and somehow still ended up marrying him. She now has two children, a nice husband, a teaching job and is still a self pitying, useless, lazy snob who looks down upon the world.

She tries to entertain herself by making snide comments and remarks about me to me. I smile back and answer her bluntly and sarcastically and get on with life.

I have come to pity the woman more than anything. I like to keep my distance as she can be rather toxic.

Next is Alan. He suffers from a mental illness. I'm not insulting the man he is actually certified. Alan's personality is that of a snobbish, selfish, vain person yet he would never have deliberately set out to cause pain or annoyance to others. Unfortunately life dealt him a rather crushing blow. Whilst at university he dropped out with depression and eventually as the paranoia set in and after numerous medications and forced stays in mental health facilities, Alan was eventually diagnosed. I had a lot of sympathy for Alan. He was intelligent, athletics, handsome and sociable with a very bright future ahead of him and suddenly everything he worked for was stolen from him and replaced with a life of fear, mistrust and mental anguish. Foe years Raymond and I had regular contact with Alan. We visited him, cleaned his house, took him shopping, visited him in hospital and went to restaurants and the cinema. He could be difficult to handle and rambled incoherently for hours yet he could also be very funny and informative and appreciative of the time we made for him. However schizophrenia rots the brain and degrades the person and changes them beyond recognition. Alan eventually became physically aggressive and physically attacked three women in two separate incidents. By this time Alan believed everyone was against him, his phone and computer were bugged and everyone including the many paramilitary groups was in on a big conspiracy to send him mad. Raymond and I had warned Alan on many occasions that the moment he lifted his hand to any of the family then all contact would be lost.

It was an autumn day when Alan kicked, punched and pushed me in front of wee Leslie that was only two years old. I contacted police made a statement and took out a non molestation and exclusion order. I couldn't trust Alan and had to protect the children. Raymond was in full agreement with my decision. We both made statements to the police. In the end the charges were withdrawn but there has never been contact with Alan since then. He has made numerous attempts to communicate through his parents but I just can't take the risk.

Before I begin may I state that Peter passed away and I do miss him.

Peter was a man that had been reared with a depressed neurotic woman and an alcoholic man.

The result was a very authoritative, austere, harsh man with very little emotion. I always felt that Peter was a man with a broken soul. He was haunted by his time at boarding school during such formative and vulnerable years. When he came home from boarding school he had lost touch with all the local children and adults and became a little reclusive. The fact that he was a control freak was his way of protecting himself. Peter had been very badly emotionally scared. The details of which no one will ever know. He never let anyone close except Winnie. However even his wife never got full access to his heart.

Peter was an emotionally disabled and was a man whom although he loved his children he never expressed his love verbally. As a father he worked very hard on the farm, provided for his children in terms of food, clothing and expenses but emotionally he starved his children.

Peter was not a bad man, he had good intentions, but then the road to hell is paved with good intentions.

There was a severe lack of communication skills with Peter and as a result he fell out with many people, simply through a lack of understanding and misunderstandings.

Peter was a very harsh and blunt man without ever trying to be hurtful. I remember on one occasion, Peter was expressing his dislike for the new island in my kitchen. He told me that "there was no way you are going to get a turkey out of that oven with that arse of yours, and let's face it it's only going to get bigger". This was a typical Peter comment. He wasn't trying to be insulting but trying or not he was usually successful.

As Raymond's wife Peter was quite accepting, he realised that I was Raymond's wife not his. He did however have trouble with Raymond and I being equals in the relationship. Peter wanted Raymond to be the boss and for me to toe the line. He couldn't understand why Raymond didn't control me. In Peter's mind if Raymond had no control over me, then I would leave him or hurt him. Again this thinking was borne out of fear on Peter's part.

For most of the time Peter and I trundled along nicely. I was aware that he was a chauvinistic control freak and he realised I was a 'fast talking' headstrong woman. That aside we helped each other out and were held together by our common ground—Raymond. We both cared about Raymond and we worked together for Raymond.

I would have fixed Peter's phone, computer or paperwork and he would babysit and treat the children. For us it worked.

However one evening I received a phone call from Peter that left me in tears and in shock. The conversion or rather ranting was that I was to drop all charges against Alan for assault or else. He told me that neither me nor my children, (i.e. his grandchildren) would ever be welcome again. He said the shame of it would be too much and that Alan was sick. At a later time he threatened to sell the farm and disown Raymond if the case went ahead. I had no choice but to withdraw the charges. It was such a difficult thing for me to do. AS a former police officer I was embarrassed at threats working and angry that I had given into intimidation. If I had been the only one threatened there is no way in hell I would have dropped the charges, however Raymond was at the heart of Peter's threats. Raymond was my Achilles heel and Peter knew it. Raymond was a 6ft tall, well built man sitting sobbing into his hands because of the hurt his father had caused. I would have done anything to take away his hurt. Peter broke Raymond's heart that day.

Over time the scars healed and Peter and I made our fragile peace. In hindsight I am so glad that we did reopen the lines of communication because a little while later it became apparent that Peter was quite ill.

He was suffering from cancer and was deteriorating quickly. I took him to hospital and sat with him for his appointments. Raymond was so worried. Eventually Peter was admitted into hospital to end his days. By now he couldn't feed himself, get to the toilet or hear. My sympathy for him was truly heartfelt. The man was dying right before my eyes and what was even sadder was that only now did Peter see and appreciate his family. He held hands with us, said how proud he was and smiled in approval. If only he had been able to see the people who loved him before.

He passed away a short time later.

Finally the dragon lady herself. Winnie! What a woman.

An evil, two faced, cold, heartless and jealous excuse for a human being. A penny pinching, mentally affected bully. I think that is a succinct description.

— By Jayne —

I first met Winnie after I had been seeing Raymond for a few months. Well my intuition was well tuned that evening. MY reaction was an insincere and very cold woman. When asked by Raymond what I thought of his mother, I said quite cold. He neither agreed nor disagreed. He wasn't defending her or offering anything to the contrary.

I never felt that Winnie was genuine or sincere. She spoke to me with her *telephone voice.* AS time went by and I spent more time at Raymond's home I realised from my observations that Winnie simply said what she thought people wanted to here. She was one person with Peter, another with Raymond, another with Alan and a different person again with Sharon. I would surmise that she was most honest and genuine with Sharon. That is disturbing because with Sharon the conversations were all about how brilliant they were and how scummy, uneducated, uncouth or useless everyone else in the town where. I don't remember them actually saying a person was really nice and leaving at that. Money really was important to Winnie. She despised people with money and looked down at those with low incomes. A woman who had never worked throughout her married life sat and condemned others because they had little money. The audacity of the woman at times was astounding.

I remember Raymond was embarrassed and hurt by his mother's reaction to the fact that my father had sexually abused me. Winnie said well Raymond that's what happens in scummy families. She told Raymond that going out with me was fine but don't let it get serious because I obviously had bad genetics. Imagine how infuriated she was when not only did I marry Raymond but I had the cheek to fall pregnant as well. To say she wasn't happy was putting mildly. I think she consoled herself with the idea that I would only have one child because apparently I wouldn't be able to cope with one. Winnie was disgusted when I fell pregnant again when Mark was only five months old. That pregnancy was poor wee Rachael who never made into this life. When Winnie was told of the miscarriage she simply said oh and genuinely couldn't understand why I would be upset. In her mind well at least than was a narrow escape.

I dropped the real clanger when I gave up my job after Jenny was born. My income was quite good and I choosing motherhood over money was simply madness. Till this day Winnie has never came to terms with the fact that I had the ability to earn a substantial wage and threw it away. My only insight is that she felt her life was somehow lacking and if she had had the chance of a career then she would have held onto it with a death grip.

We trudged along, me annoying her and vice versa. Then came the assault by Alan. Winnie was the stirrer and Peter was her front man. She made the balls and he fired them. Winnie orchestrated and was totally behind the masterminding of Peter's threats. She had told friends and colleagues that Alan was living in Belfast and working as a journalist. The truth was he was a mentally ill, living in a dirty hovel on benefits, with previous assault charges against women. She said that if the truth got out she could never show her face again. If she hadn't put up such a pretence to others there would be no shame but sympathy from others.

When Peter became sick is when Winnie disgusted me the most. I had listened for years to her ridicule people including me, snipe and jibe, stir trouble, con and deceive but her depths of inhumanity were about to be revealed in all their glory.

Peter was a hard working man who always financially provided for his family. Prior to getting sick he was the boss and that was that, Winnie did as she was told. Then when she smelled weakness she pounced. I had to take Peter to a lot of appointments and he told me how lonely he was and how scared to be on his own. I informed Winnie of his fears and she told me that she wasn't a nurse and if Peter wanted a nurse he should have married one. She never missed a day at her job, not through dedication but greed for money and lack of sympathy. Whilst Peter was in hospital for diagnostic tests which took four weeks, Winnie refused to visit him and resented having to bring him home at the weekends. IT was too expensive to drive to the hospital and anyway she was tired. At one point she even claimed the Peter enjoyed his stay in hospital. When we went to visit Peter he was so happy to see a face but would never let us stay long because he wouldn't have wanted to be a burden.

Raymond had a word with his mother and made it clear that this was the beginning of the end for Peter and to enjoy every minute she had with him. Her response was that she was enjoying the peace. After the diagnostic tests Peter came home. He was very weak at this point and needed cared for. Winnie remained resolute that she would not be altering her life. He use to beg me to come and visit when she had left for work because he was so lonely. I also had to smuggle in food because Winnie wouldn't buy anything and Peter could no longer get to the shops. She even refused to get him his brand of toothpaste as it was too expensive. A few weeks passed and Peter continued to deteriorate. Winnie now refused to put on the heating as it was simply burning money. However she left on one gas heater during the day and at night Peter had to sleep alone in a freezing cold room. You could actually see your breath in the room. I wouldn't have let a dog sleep there never mind a dying man, her husband of many years. Not surprisingly Peter took a severe chest infection and almost died one night. The next day he was taken into hospital with a very poor prognosis.

During his last hospital stay I went and visited during the day and made sure he was fed and washed as he could no longer control his hands. Winnie reluctantly went down at night and complained relentlessly about it. May I point out that still she hadn't taken time off work? Work by the way is a very unimportant administration role in a very slow office.

During one of my visits with Peter he asked to get home and he cried. That was the saddest moment throughout his illness. The man had been reduced to begging. Under no circumstances would Winnie bring him home, despite a care package and facilities in place. I offered to bring him to my home and care for him for his last days but she refused point blank. I just could not understand how cold she was. At one point she told me that since he wasn't going to get any better it would be good if he died sooner rather than later because it was exhausting running to a hospital and that the inconvenience had interfered with her soap viewing. I was angry and speechless.

The last six days of Peter's life was spent in intensive care with the possibility that he would die at anytime. Raymond desperately wanted to stay with Peter but he also had a farm to run and we had three young children. Raymond and I decided to come down about six in the evening and stay all night till nine in the morning. That way if Peter had a bad night we were there to help and the thought of him dying alone was unthinkable. Even this annoyed Winnie. Not only did she not want to care for Peter but she didn't want us to either. At one point she informed me that we weren't actually allowed to stay, in some petty attempt to deter us.

Peter had a very bad night and although Raymond had to go home I said I would stay with Winnie that day because he was in such a poor way. That evening at five o'clock Peter passed away as peacefully as possible. I broke down and cried, cried for Peter and cried for Raymond's loss and the loss of the children's beloved Papa. Winnie never dropped a tear and couldn't wait till get home. I had to force her to ring Sharon and Alan.

At home that night all she could discuss was how good it would be not to have to go back to the hospital. I suggested to, go back and thank the nurse who cared for him. I was met with a hard solid no. Needless to say I returned a few days later and thanked the staff.

Putting the death notices in the papers pained her greatly due to the cost, buying flowers was apparently unnecessary and she hoped no one would come to the wake because she couldn't be bothered. Still no tears.

Peter's had a favourite song that he whistled it and sang it ever since I met him and he had taught Raymond how to play it on the piano. I suggested that we play it at the funeral as the lyrics are very appropriate. Winnie said she never heard him sing that in her life. She was deliberately trying to be as obstreperous as possible. The wake and funeral was tough going but we got through it. From that day to this I can never forget how she treated a dying helpless man, the father of her children whom she was married to for forty years. I quickly discovered significant sum written for personal use. This seems fine until I realised the personal use items were for Sharon not any members of the farm. Winnie was screwing over Raymond financially. It's no wonder she tried to avoid giving me the books. As I have a degree in accountancy the irregularities were obvious.

Then came the will. She tried to refuse to pay for the funeral and sulked that she was left a pittance for all her years. I thought she was married to Peter not employed by him. She was looking for a severance package. Money occupied her mind not grief. Raymond was ashamed of her.

Raymond and I pay all her household bills as we know Peter would have liked her taken care of and this is apparently still not good enough.

I don't know how to keep her happy and have given up trying.

At present she watches my every move, snipes at me, pities Raymond for being married to me and rants because I am not in paid employment. The fact that I rear her grandchildren and help run the business to pay her bills is apparently of no consequence.

Raymond's granny had a saying that I believe has a lot of truth in it;

If you want to get along with folk, have nothing to do with them.

I think I will be taking her advice from now on.

God

THIS IS A DELICATE AREA. Have you ever noticed that as soon as the God word comes up in conversation, people in this so called Christian country, become very uncomfortable and would pay to be anywhere but with you.

I am not a raving bible basher or a street preacher on a soap box; however I do have a strong belief in God. I shouldn't have to feel ashamed about the fact, yet I do feel that I always have to explain myself. Prove that I haven't lost my marbles.

Throughout my childhood I knew that what I was suffering was traumatic and devastating yet I never blamed god. I never asked why me or how could you let this happen. Instead I felt that this was my life set out before me and God was not deserting me, but rather walking with me through life. I take great comfort from the prayer *Footprints in the Sand*. (Shown on the next page.) At low times, of which there where an abundance, when I felt that I couldn't go on, it was my belief in God that kept me strong. The belief that suicide would rule out heaven and meeting my granny was also what helped keep me alive. Although I was born into a mixed religion marriage, (Catholic & Protestant), I was never taken to Chapel or Church, except for big events. We never had a bible in the house and at school I zoned out during RE as I couldn't relate to Sundays Mass. I received my first bible, the Gideon bible, during secondary school. I valued the book and stored it away safely. Strangely though, I always had an inherent belief in a greater being, a purpose for each life and a sense of good overthrowing evil. Romantic ideals perhaps but I believed in them and I still do.

Footprints Prayer
Footprints in the Sand

One night I had a dream . . .
I dreamed I was walking along the beach with the Lord, and
Across the sky flashed scenes from my life.
For each scene I noticed two sets of footprints in the sand;
One belonged to me, and the other to the Lord.
When the last scene of my life flashed before us,
I looked back at the footprints in the sand.
I noticed that many times along the path of my life,
There was only one set of footprints.
I also noticed that it happened at the very lowest and saddest
times in my life
This really bothered me, and I questioned the Lord about it.
"Lord, you said that once I decided to follow you,
You would walk with me all the way;
But I have noticed that during the most troublesome times in
my life,
There is only one set of footprints.
I don't understand why in times when I needed you the most,
you should leave me.
The Lord replied, "My precious, precious child. I love you, and
I would never, never leave you during your times of trial and
suffering.
When you saw only one set of footprints,
It was then that I carried you."

~~~~~~

Footprints Prayer

I have noticed that as the world becomes more affluent and better educated, people are starting to almost demand proof that God exists. I don't need proof because I know I believe and that's all I need to know. I am not going to argue that every word in the bible has been accurately translated or that every passage should be taken literally. The bible is a living book that will continue to educate and feed your soul with every read. I know with all my being that there is a greater power, the creator and protector. I believe in a spiritual God who walks with us through our lives, and is waiting for us to reach out to him.

I am a member of the Presbyterian Church since university and recently I had attended a number of events and worship evenings at the local Baptist Church. The congregation at both Churches are welcoming and inviting, and I enjoy each in its own right. However it is strange that Baptists are deemed as bible bashers or saved and therefore loopy, yet the more mainstream Presbyterians are upstanding respectable people. Each Church believes in the same God, read the same bible and believe that we are all sinners unworthy of God's love and mercy. It is strange how frightened people are of the one man who died to save them.

I don't like having to justify my beliefs and would never dream to criticise another religion. I am aware of my values and beliefs and only need to justify them to God.

I have in the past tried to go at the 'God issue' from another angle, from the scientific aspect. Yet no matter how much I read about the absence of proof that God exists, I have always been drawn back to my deeply held belief in God. I don't profess my faith in any religion but in God, and God alone. I don't need justification for my beliefs; God was through life with me and is there when I need him most.

I want to live my life in his image. I know and accept that I am a sinner and every day I disappoint Jesus by sinning in thought, word or deed.

I am very far from perfect. I swear too much, let my anger boil up at times, can be very critical and at times place too much emphasis on unimportant things in life. I am a sinner, but a sinner who believes in God and a sinner who tries my best each day to be worthy of God's love.

My future

CRAZY AS IT MAY SEEM I am more positive about my future than I have ever been before. Writing this book has helped immensely. As a person with OCD getting all my thoughts, memories and ramblings down on paper frees up my mind. It has been a very painful experience to lay my life bare in black and white, but equally it is something I needed to do. I have lived through hell, crawled out the other side and somehow managed to build a life for myself. I have gained an education, completed my degree, and experienced my ideal job as a police officer. I have be blessed with meeting a fantastic man who helped me create three wonderful, joy giving children who I would give my life for. My current life is no big shakes but for me it is a blissful oasis in life's desert.

I am trying to make sense of my life so far and find some peace and sense of order before I continue on the next leg of my journey. I need to ground myself, shower my head, and face the second half of my life revitalised and reinvigorated. I know that depression and I are firm friends with regular catch up meetings yet I am also learning to live with this unwanted guest rather than fight with it. Winston Churchill aptly personified depression as *The Black Dog*. It is a large, angry dog that appears from nowhere and cannot be shooed away.

I have been mentally scarred by my childhood experiences and carry with me nightmares, self loathing, insecurities and vivid recollections that can be triggered by something as insignificant as a smell. I however have powerful weapons in my support arsenal—Raymond, David, Jenny, and Leslie, my sister Diana, a few very close friends and God. With them by my side I know that I will have the strength to overcome the large, deep, black pools of depression that interrupt my travel through life.

Death I hope is in the distant future, yet I don't fear death. I know that I will be in God's capable hands and will be called home once more. I rejoice in the anticipation of holding my little Rachael and can't imagine ever letting go of her. Until that time comes I know my granny (mammy), will love and care for Rachael.

Conclusion

I AM LOOKING FORWARD TO completing my life's work; the rearing of my children to the best of my ability.

I have one wish for each of my children, and as they grow and mature and develop the individual personalities then my wish will take on different meaning for each one. I wish with all my heart that they will be *happy—truly happy.*

They are my life's work and I love my job.

With God's help I will survive the life sentence bestowed upon me by my parents and serve out the remainder of my days.